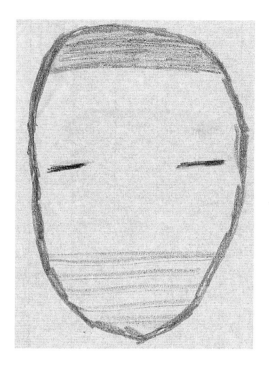

"Somewhere God has a home,
Because God's place is huge,
So big you know it's the universe;
And that means
You enter his home
When you're born
And you stay there
After you die—you're not gone."

—Rebecca, nine years old

"You can't find God someplace.
He's everywhere.
All places—the ocean,
land, the sky.
His church is everyone,
Everything—he made
us all, and it all, too.
But I'll try to find a home for him."

— Colin, eleven years old

In God's House

Children's Drawings

Compiled with a Foreword by

Robert Coles

WILLIAM B. EERDMANS PUBLISHING COMPANY

Grand Rapids, Michigan

Cambridge, U.K.

The publisher and Dr. Coles wish to thank the children from Wedgewood Christian Youth and Family Services and Heartside Ministries of Grand Rapids, Michigan, and the children living in Brazil who participated in this project. The identities of several of the children remain anonymous to respect their request for confidentiality. Fictitious names have been given to these children.

William B. Eerdmans Publishing Company
Grand Rapids, Michigan

Printed in Mexico

00 99 98 97 96   7 6 5 4 3 2 1

Library of Congress Cataloging-in-Publication Data
In God's House : drawings by children / compiled by Robert Coles.
p.   cm.
Summary: Drawings and comments by various poor, sick, abandoned,
or abused children present their views of God and where God lives.
ISBN 0-8028-5126-6 (alk. paper)
1. Children— Religious life.   2. God — Juvenile literature.
3. Presence of God — Juvenile literature.   4. Children's drawings — Psychological aspects.
[1. God   2. Children's art.   3. Children's writings.]   I. Coles, Robert.
BV4571.2.I5   1996
200' .83 — dc20   95-53990
*   CIP*
*   AC*

ISBN 0-8028-5126-6

Designed by Joy Chu

"I picture God on a throne.
He's King of all the people.
He tries to keep track of us.
But remember:
He told us
We have to look after ourselves.
That's important, you know."
— Josephine, nine years old

Foreword *by Robert Coles*

For over thirty years I have talked with children
about their lives, their hopes and worries, their wishes and fears. I
started doing so in Children's Hospital of Boston, Massachusetts,
where I learned first to be a pediatrician and then a child
psychiatrist. Later I became a so-called "field worker," a doctor
whose job it was to interview young people in schools and in their
homes. That work took me all over the United States and abroad.
It enabled me to get to know children "of all sorts and conditions"
— poor children and reasonably well-off children and quite well-to-
do children, white children and black children, children who lived
in cities and children who lived in small towns and the countryside,
children on Indian reservations and in Eskimo villages and in the
slums of Brazil.

From the very start of my work, I asked children to draw
pictures. I had discovered that a boy or girl who is drawing or
painting is a person trying to say something, trying to show what is
on his or her mind. Indeed, I will never forget being told by an
eight-year-old girl who was dying of leukemia what a particular
drawing meant to her. The picture showed grass and flowers,
carefully drawn, covering an entire piece of fairly large-sized paper.

"That's God," she said.

I was a bit taken aback, and though I didn't say anything right away, she guessed my surprise, my confusion, and so she readily explained her thinking: "I'll soon be meeting Him, the Lord, and that's where we'll meet, maybe."

I was, at that moment, both instructed by and more than a little in awe of this child — her brave candor, her lively imagination. She was in great medical danger. She knew she'd soon die. She had every intention of letting me, her doctor, know that she was fully alert to her situation — but that she was looking ahead with a certain hopefulness. God would greet her on a big green meadow, filled with flowers of all colors, kinds, and sizes.

I was anxious to discover where God actually was in that drawing, so I asked her indirectly. "I don't see God there."

She took my literal-minded, unimaginative inquiry quite in stride. "Oh, you might not see God, maybe — He'll just whisper to you. He's like the wind. You'll see — I'll see — all the flowers bend, I hope, and that way, I'll know He's there, smiling on us."

Now, I wanted to know about "us." I indicated my curiosity by repeating the word with a slight raising of my voice. "Us?"

"The flowers and me," I was told.

A girl had shared with me a big leap of sorts, a moral leap. Out of all the suffering she had experienced, some "good" would soon enough take place — her arrival in a version of the land of milk and honey, there to feel in the presence of a God who in her mind is formless, yet unmistakably *there*, as real and elusive as the wind.

So it goes, similarly, for the children whose pictures make up this book. Like that girl, they are also "at risk" — for one reason or another they are poor, hurt, ailing, abandoned, abused, victims of bad luck. Like her (like all children, actually), they are struggling to make sense of this world, and of their situation in it.

Many of the "whys" children ask are here rendered pictorially. These children who are living at the edge, as it were, have surely wondered not only why that is so, but when their luck might change. God, for them (as for many adults who are believers in Him), offers the possibility of a change in that luck. Picture after picture and statement after statement tells us where He is, where He lives, and that in His "home" one will find freedom, beauty, plentiful food, great strength, love, and, not least, a "place" where moral distinctions are made and where they count — a kind of justice, that is.

On the other hand, as a twelve-year-old boy lets us know, such awesome power and authority as the Lord's can prompt nervousness, the fear of divine judgment: "It is a scary place. I'm scared to draw this."

Not that these children only seek a better life in the next world. They let their imaginations have full reign. They ask us to shed our earthbound, daily lives — to soar, with them, into a symbolically charged realm, informed by fantasy and magic, both of which are a child's natural allies.

In a Brazilian slum, three children of one family conjure up

God's home. One child draws a field of flowers guarded by two crosses, two trees, with night and day living side by side, all for God to enjoy. Another draws a thick stretch of earth with the cross on it, placed in the sky. There are red arrows from the sun and a rainbow to suggest aspects of God's life, His "energy." And there are the mountains of Rio de Janeiro with a famous statue of Jesus on one of them — a reminder of this earthly life, which looks relatively insignificant compared to the "upper" or heavenly one. A third child takes that same statue of Jesus, which dominates the Brazilian city, and connects it to the sky and the sun — to eternity, perhaps. All of this is suggested with splashes of color: a mix of the literal, the here-and-now, and the infinite.

In their own provocative ways, these children join their parents and teachers, their elders — showing with crayons and responsive comments how powerfully God informs their lives and prompts from them speculation, creative exploration, and expression. Their minds are eager to fathom the world's mysteries, including those of faith — or of what lies ahead in God's scheme of things.

John, twelve years old

"This is a ladder going up to the clouds.
When you get through the clouds,
here is the path to God's house."

Daniel, twelve years old

"The house is gold. It is beautiful
inside. There are two suns, because
everyone is going to be happy. All
the people are happy. There is a
house with free stuff inside.
Everyone will get rewards. Everyone
will be rich. There is a tree, grass,
and a river, because these things
make people happy. I am smiling. I
am free. Everyone is free."

I 'AM fRee.

We All ARe fRee.

free stuff

Gold.

Gold.

We're come's God home And for you

God will you be

Gold

Well come

Gold.

I 'AM so hAPPely

Yes, Cool.

Tim, twelve years old

"These are clouds. This is a picture
of God. God is always with us."

"I want to draw a church. I want it to be perfect. I'm drawing what God made — a flower. God made his own house. It's a pretty good house. This is where he keeps his bad people—bad prisoners. I'm making a garden. This is his garden. It's where he grows his food. He grows food for everyone. There will be enough food for everyone. I'm drawing a welcome sign. I want it to say 'Welcome to All Children.'"

Sarah, twelve years old

"The ground is going to be gold. There will be a lot of trees. There are two pearls as gates with angels guarding them. There is a big old throne where God sits but we can't see God's face, because he's too bright. There are angels all around the throne. They are singing, 'O mighty God, we worship you!' The angels have halos and you can't see their faces. You cannot pass the gate, because the angels are guarding it with swords. This is hell. It is a lake. It's red, because it's fire. All the people are happy, because they have smiles on their faces."

Lue, eight years old

"God lives in Heaven and in my house."

Mariah, four years old

"I think of flowers when I think of God."

Carl, twelve years old

"God lives in heaven above the clouds.
His house is a big castle. Jesus is
standing there. It is a scary place.
I'm scared to draw this."

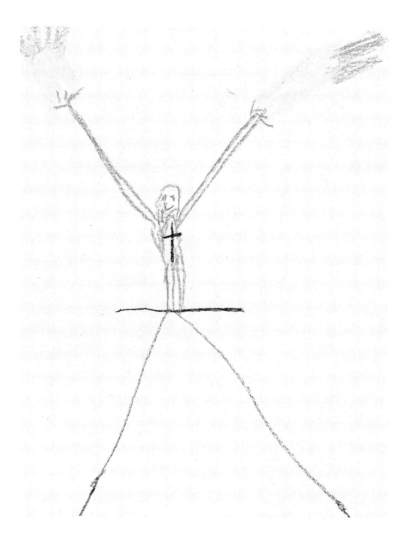

Eduardo, eight years old

"Jesus Christ lives on a mountain higher than any mountains here [on earth], and [he] gives us sun and he gives us the sky, and he gives us our faith in him, and that [last gift] is the biggest [one]."

Carlos, twelve years old

"God keeps us alive by the sun.
Without the sun, we'd die. The sun
shines over everyone, even if you are
poor. God likes rainbows — he visits
us that way. Where he lives, it's bigger
than anything you can see; it's strong;
it's mighty strong."

"Up in the sky, there's this place, and God is there, and he likes flowers and trees and he looks at the stars and the sun, and you can't see him, but he can see you, and if you're a good person, he shines on you with his sun and he twinkles on you with his stars."

Derek, eight years old

"You don't see God,
You don't hear him,
You know him.
That means, he beats
When your heart beats,
He's in your head,
You think of him,
So you're not lonely,
Not when your prayers
Bring him home.
His home is in you!"

—Alice, twelve years old

"God is living in all the planets.
The sky is where he lives—
The sun, too.
I don't know what his
Voice would sound like.
Everyone would listen, though."

— Ned, ten years old

"He has this big house, God does, and he has a room for everyone who comes there, and he shines on you."

— Mary, eight years old

"God—you can't see him, but he's the light of the world. He rules us."

— Timothy, eleven years old